Our Family

A Keepsake Album

LION
Giftlines

This edition copyright © 2000 Lion Publishing
Illustrations copyright © 2000 Elizabeth Harbour

Published by
Lion Publishing plc
Sandy Lane West, Oxford, England
www.lion-publishing.co.uk
ISBN 0 7459 4201 6

First edition 2000
10 9 8 7 6 5 4 3 2 1 0

Acknowledgments
Pages 9, 11, 25, 33, 34, 42: Isaiah 8:18,
I John 4:7, Ruth 1:16, Matthew 18:5, John
16:22, Ecclesiastes 9:10, quoted from the
Good News Bible published by The Bible
Societies/HarperCollins Publishers Ltd, UK
© American Bible Society 1966, 1971, 1976,
1992, used with permission.

Spelling and punctuation of quotations
may have been modernized.

A catalogue record for this book is available
from the British Library

Typeset in Berkeley OldStyle
Printed and bound in Singapore

A keepsake of the

.... *family*

Introduction

We choose our friends, but we're given our family.

A family is a unique blend of generations, ages and personalities. With care, it can become an environment in which each person is valued and appreciated and where everyone can learn from each other.

Each family has its own way of doing things. As the years go by, it establishes traditions, coins its own sayings and builds up a treasury of stories and memories.

This book is designed to help you capture some of the spirit of your family history. Write in it and make it your own. There are suggestions as to what you might include, but there is also plenty of space to add photographs, notes and memorabilia. In this way, the album will become a record that you and your children will want to keep and to pass on to future generations. A record of a unique group of people – your family.

The sun shines warmer at home.
Albanian proverb

There's no place like home.
L. Frank Baum

Contents

Our Family

Our family tree 6

Immediate family 8

Close relatives 10

Relatives and friends 12

A family likeness 14

What's in a name? 16

Our Home

Home sweet home 18

Childhood memories 20

Where we used to live 22

Home and abroad 24

Holidays 26

Anniversaries

Birthdays 28

Weddings 30

Births 32

Deaths 34

Daily Life

Work 36

Schools 38

Hobbies 40

Achievements 42

Traditions 44

Thoughts 46

Our family tree

Great-grandfather

Date of birth

                    Grandfather

                    Date of birth

Great-grandmother

Date of birth

Great-grandfather

Date of birth

                    Grandmother

                    Date of birth

Great-grandmother

Date of birth

Great-grandfather

Date of birth

                    Grandfather

                    Date of birth

Great-grandmother

Date of birth

Great-grandfather

Date of birth

                    Grandmother

                    Date of birth

Great-grandmother

Date of birth

Father

Date of birth

Children

Date of birth

Mother

Date of birth

Immediate family

Make this page a family gallery, with photographs, names and dates of birth.

*Tell me whom you
live with, and I will
tell you who you are.*
Spanish proverb

Here I am, with the children the Lord has given me.

From the Old Testament book of Isaiah

Close relatives

Make this a record of some of your closest relatives:
grandfathers and grandmothers, aunts and uncles.

*Children need the wisdom of their elders;
the ageing need the encouragement of a
child's exuberance.*
Author unknown

Dear friends, let us love one another.

From the New Testament
first letter of John

Relatives and friends

Here is space to include pictures and details of your wider family and friends.

Relationships are the place where the work of life happens.
Mike Yaconelli

*Happy is the house
that shelters a friend.*
Ralph Waldo Emerson

*Personal relations are
the important thing
for ever and ever.*
E.M. Forster

A family likeness

It's fun to trace the family resemblance. Who looks like whom in the family? Compare photos, including names, ages and the dates the photos were taken.

An apple cleft in two is not more twin
Than these two creatures.

William Shakespeare

What's in a name?

Many names have a meaning. Find out what the first names and surnames in your family mean.

*The best and most
beautiful things in the
world cannot be seen
or touched but are felt
in the heart.*

Helen Keller

*What's in a name?
That which we call a rose
By any other name would
smell as sweet.*

William Shakespeare

17

Home sweet home

Whether you live in a mansion or a tiny basement flat, the place you call home is your own space, where you can relax and simply be yourself. The following pages allow you to focus on family homes, both past and present.

Home is… where the heart is.

Home is… where you can find your way in the dark.

Home is… where the great are small and the small are great.

Childhood memories

I remember, I remember,
The house where I was born,
The little window where the sun
Came peeping in at morn.
Thomas Hood

Give details of places that were important to you when you were young.
There is space to include photographs.

Wherever you are, you should always be contented, but especially at home, because there you must spend the most of your time.
Jane Austen

Where we used to live

List some of the places where your family has lived,
with the dates of when you lived there.

*These are the walls that
kept our family safe,
Saw our tears and heard
our laughter.*
Author unknown

Happiness is to be found only in the home where each one loves, and helps, and cares for the others.
Theophanes Vénard

23

Home and abroad

It's fascinating to find out about places where people have lived or travelled to. Find out where members of your family have been. Give details of who they were and why they went, how they travelled and how long it took.

Where'er I roam,
whatever realms to see,
My heart untravelled
fondly turns to thee.
Oliver Goldsmith

Wherever you go, I will go;
wherever you live, I will live.
Your people will be my people,
and your God will be my God.
From the Old Testament book of Ruth

Holidays

Here is space to record memorable family holidays,
with photos and details of where you went and when.

Now I am in a holiday humour.

William Shakespeare

And young and old come forth to play
On a sunshine holiday.

John Milton

Anniversaries

Birthdays

Write it on your heart that every day is the best day of the year.
Ralph Waldo Emerson

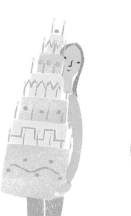

A birthday is not a celebration of the year that is past, but of the year that is about to begin.

Mike Yaconelli

Weddings

So we grew together,
Two lovely berries moulded on one stem;
So, with two seeming bodies, but one heart.

William Shakespeare

The old order changeth,
yielding place to new,
And God fulfils himself
in many ways.
Alfred, Lord Tennyson

Anniversaries

Births

'Do you know who made you?'
'Nobody, as I knows on,'
said the child, with a short laugh…
'I 'spect I grow'd.'
Robert Louis Stevenson

32

Whoever welcomes in my name
one such child as this, welcomes me.
From the New Testament gospel of Matthew

Anniversaries

Deaths

Now you are sad,
but I will see you again,
and your hearts will be
filled with gladness.

From the New Testament gospel of John

The holiest of all holidays are those
Kept by ourselves in silence and apart;
The secret anniversaries of the heart.
Henry Wadsworth Longfellow

35

Daily Life

Work

It can be very interesting to trace all the different things family members have done. Here is space to record some details about family occupations, past and present. If you have any pictures or memorabilia, add them too.

There is scarcely any less bother
in the running of a family than
in that of an entire state.
Michel Eyquem de Montaigne

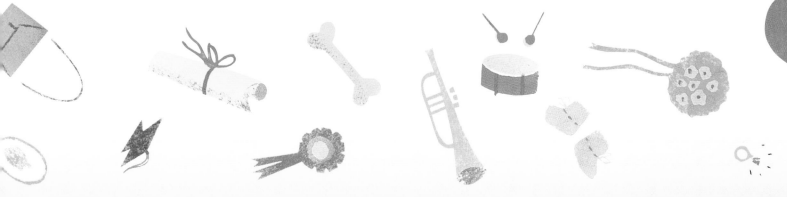

Daily Life

Schools

List the schools which have educated members of your family over the years. Include your favourite school photos.

Education has for its object the formation of character.
Herbert Spencer

… The whining schoolboy, with his satchel,
And shining morning face, creeping like snail
Unwillingly to school.
William Shakespeare

Hobbies

One of the pleasures of family life is seeing how each individual becomes captivated by a particular interest: sport, art, music, literature, food, crafts, games… Use these pages to record who enjoys doing what in your family. There's plenty of space for photos and mementoes too.

Games, pastimes and hobbies of all kinds should be encouraged.
Isabella Beeton

Believe me, my young friend, there is nothing – absolutely nothing – half so much worth doing as simply messing about in boats.
Kenneth Grahame

41

Achievements

Sometimes it's good to blow the family trumpet. Here is space to record achievements of all kinds – details of competitions, qualifications, certificates, cups or medals, as well as groups or activities that family members have been involved with.

Work hard at whatever you do.

From the Old Testament book of Ecclesiastes

Let us, then, be up and doing,
With a heart for any fate;
Still achieving, still pursuing,
Learn to labour and to wait.

Henry Wadsworth Longfellow

Daily Life
Traditions

I am the family face;
Flesh perishes, I live on,
Projecting trait and trace
Through time to times anon.
Thomas Hardy

Every family has its stories and traditions, some more
unusual than others. Record some of yours here. Future
generations will then know where it all began!

*Every generation
revolts against its
fathers and makes
friends with its
grandfathers.*
Lewis Mumford

45

Thoughts

Peace be to this house and to all who dwell in it.
Peace be to them that enter and to them that depart.

The Book of Common Prayer

All shall be well, and all shall be well,
and all manner of things shall be well.

Julian of Norwich

If there is righteousness in the heart,
there will be beauty in the character.
If there is beauty in the character,
there will be harmony in the home.
If there is harmony in the home,
there will be order in the nation.
When there is order in each nation,
there will be peace in the world.

Chinese proverb

East, west, home's best.

Traditional